ROOSTERS

DIANA WEBB

Lily's Lollipop Wand

illustrated by
Anni Axworthy

HODDER AND STOUGHTON
London Sydney Auckland Toronto

CINDERELLA
OLD
ROAD
SCHOOL

British Library Cataloguing in Publication Data

Webb, Diana
Lily's lollipop wand.
I. Title II. Axworthy, Anni
823'.914 [J]

ISBN 0-340-42282-3

First published 1988

Published by Hodder and Stoughton Children's Books,
a division of Hodder and Stoughton Ltd,
Mill Road, Dunton Green, Sevenoaks, Kent TN13 2YJ

Photoset in Great Britain by En to En,
Tunbridge Wells, Kent

Printed in Great Britain by T. J. Press (Padstow) Ltd,
Padstow, Cornwall

1 The Pantomime

There was great excitement at Old Road School. It was Christmas, and this year the grown-ups were doing a pantomime for the children. Lily the lollipop lady was taking part, of course. There was one part that only Lily could play. The pantomime, chosen with Lily in mind, was Cinderella. Lily was playing the fairy godmother and her lollipop the wand.

The rehearsals were fun. Class One's pet mice were in the pantomime. Lily had to wave her lollipop over them. The lights went out. Someone made a flash.
And when the lights came on again a giant rocking-horse was there instead.

Lennie, the retired lollipop man from over the hill, was lending his prize pumpkin. Lily had to wave her lollipop

over it. Then the lights went out again. Someone made another flash. And when the lights came on a carriage built specially by Lennie was there instead.

And a teacher who had just got married was lending her wedding dress. She played Cinderella. At the start she wore rags. Lily had to wave her lollipop over her. Then the lights went out for the third time. Someone made a third flash. And when the lights came on the teacher was wearing the wedding dress.

Lily loved pretending to make Cinderella's wishes come true. But of course it was only pretending. The magic in the pantomime was all done by tricks. And that made Lily sad.

For Lily knew that at Christmas time children are like Cinderella. They long for things and make wishes. She knew that most children at Old Road School would see their wishes come true. Their mums and dads would just go to the shops and buy the things they longed for. But she also knew that many children would not be so lucky. Many children would get no presents at all. That was why Lily felt sad. She loved all children. She wanted to make those children's wishes come true as well, so they could have presents on Christmas morning, too.

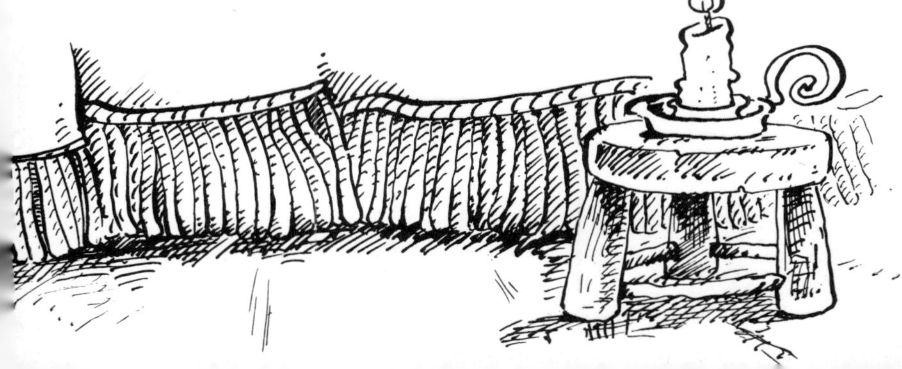

Lily spoke to her lollipop. 'I can do so many wonderful things with you,' she said. 'But if I could use you to provide toys for children who won't be getting any, that would be the best thing of all.'

Standing in her living-room at home Lily tried.

'Now what would lots of those children like?' she said, waving her lollipop. 'From out of thin air a shiny new bike!' But of course nothing happened.

She tried again. 'What would make other children happy? A doll that cries and wets its nappy!' But once again nothing happened.

'It's no good,' sighed Lily. 'You can't help to grant needy children's Christmas wishes, lollipop. You're not really magic and you never will be.'

STOP
HILDREN

2 **Dress Rehearsal**

One day soon afterwards, Lily was reading the newspaper. Suddenly something in the paper caught her eye. She read it again. She read it carefully many times. Then slowly she put the paper down. She lifted her lollipop.

'Oh, lollipop,' she gasped, 'I think perhaps you could make a lot of those children's wishes come true after all. But it would mean . . .'

Lily gulped. She clutched the lollipop tightly. She read the piece in the paper a dozen more times. Then she stared at her lollipop. It shook in her hand. Her legs went wobbly and she had a lump in her throat.

STOP
CHILDREN
STOP
CHILDREN
FINISH
STOP
CHILDREN

'But then perhaps that's why I've hung on to you so tightly all this time,' she whispered. 'Perhaps I've just been saving you and making you famous so that you can do the most wonderful thing of all.'

Lily took a very deep breath. 'I'll do something about it now,' she said. 'I'll have to do it now.'

Very slowly and deliberately she walked to the telephone. With a trembling finger she dialled a number. And with a trembling voice she said what she had to say.

That night it was the final dress rehearsal of the pantomime. Two children, Sammy and Susie Squiffins, were there, helping their dad with the scenery.

'Dress rehearsals always go wrong,' said Sammy. 'My mum says so.' And this dress rehearsal did go wrong. Lily was dressed in a sparkly dress and cloak. Her lollipop was bound in shiny silver ribbon and had a silver star stuck on top. But Lily couldn't concentrate. She got her words mixed up.

'You shall not go to the prince's great ball,' she said to Cinderella. 'No, instead you shall stay in the hearth after all.'

That's not like Lily, thought Sammy Squiffins. Perhaps something's bothering her.

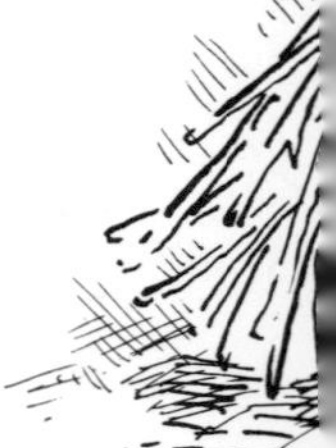

STOP
CHILDREN

Then one of the mice escaped from its cage. Lily screamed and ran all round the stage.

That's not like Lily either, thought Sammy. I'm sure something's bothering her.

Then Lily carelessly brushed her lollipop against a lighted candle. The lollipop wand was on fire!

'Oh, no,' cried Lily in panic. 'No one will want it if it's damaged. No one will want it then.'

Fortunately it was only a little fire. It was quickly put out and the lollipop was fine.

But that's not like Lily at all, thought Sammy Squiffins. Something is definitely bothering her. And I'm going to find out what it is.

3 **The Auction**

After the rehearsal, Sammy and Susie followed Lily home. Lily felt tears in her eyes. She took a hanky from her pocket to wipe them and a piece of newspaper fell out.

Sammy Squiffins crept to pick it up. GRAND CHARITY AUCTION it said.

'What's an auction?' said Susie, reading over his shoulder.

Sammy scratched his head. 'I think it's when lots of people want to buy the same thing. And the person who can pay the most gets it,' he said. They read on. The piece of paper said that the next day there was to be a big sale of things that belonged to famous people.

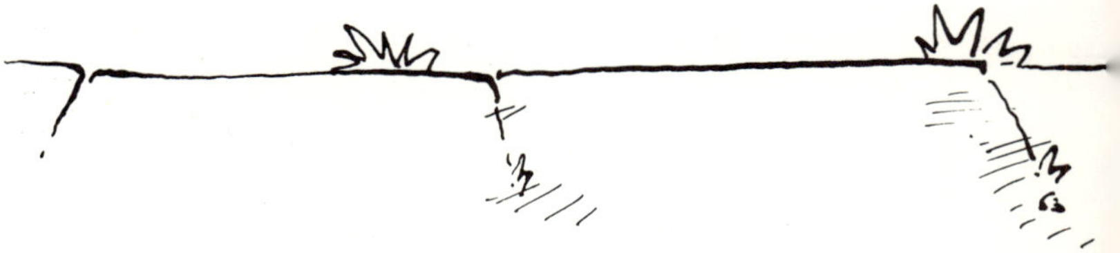

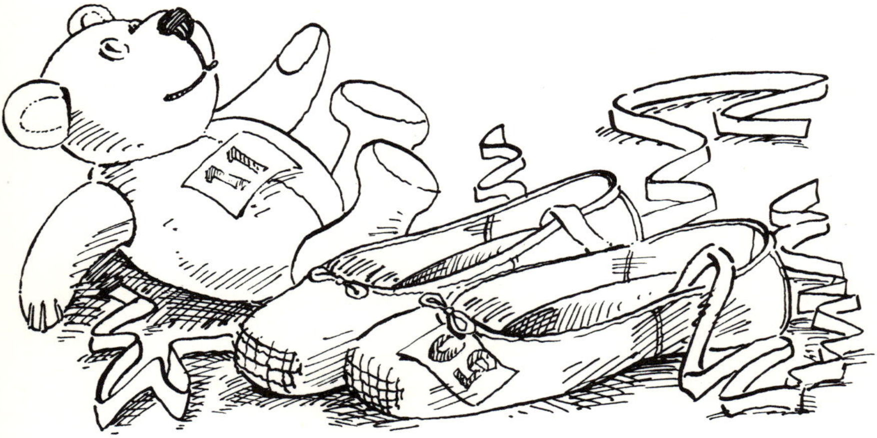

Susie looked at Sammy. 'Lily's famous,' she said. 'She's famous for all those lollipop pictures she painted and all those lollipop dances she danced.'

They read further. It said the Prime Minister was giving an old teddy bear to be sold. A ballerina was giving some ballet shoes. An author was giving an old typewriter. And it would be an auction. The people who wanted to give the most money for the things would get them. And all the money would be used to buy Christmas presents for children in need.

Sammy and Susie looked at each other.

'She keeps saying she'd like her lollipop to grant real wishes,' said Susie.

'Yes, and she said no one would want it if it was damaged,' gasped Sammy.

'She must be giving it to the auction then!' they both gasped together. 'She's giving away her famous lollipop. Some people might give a lot of money to buy that!'

Sammy and Susie were dismayed. They both thought hard.

'Whatever are we going to do?' they said at last. Then they both nodded. 'There's only one thing we can do,' they agreed.

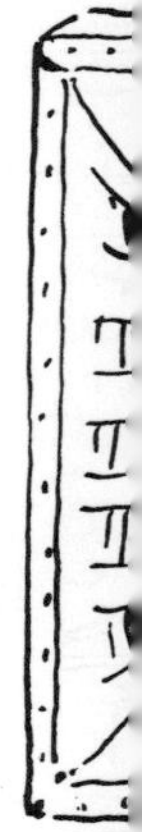

The next morning Sammy and Susie turned up at the Grand Charity Auction. There was no sign of Lily. But they could see her lollipop propped up with the other things that were being sold.

Susie turned out her purse. 'I've got two pounds fifty,' she said. 'That's my pocket money, the money Uncle Joe sent for Christmas and two lots from the tooth fairy.'

Sammy turned out his pockets. 'I've got one pound seventy-five,' he said. 'That's my pocket money, the money from Uncle Joe and ten pence I found in the street.'

The auction began. The teddy bear was sold first. Then the ballet shoes and the typewriter were sold. They went for hundreds of pounds. People kept putting their hands up. Higher and higher prices were called.

Then it was the turn of Lily's lollipop. The man at the front described it. He said it had belonged to Lily, the famous lollipop lady, and it had royal fingerprints on it, too.

'Four pounds five pence,' called Sammy, waving their money in the air.

'No,' hissed Susie. 'You can't add up. It's four pounds twenty-five.'

But someone else was already calling 'Fifty pounds.' Then someone was calling 'A hundred.'

'It's no good,' signed Sammy sadly. 'No good at all.'

4 **The Wrong Wand**

That evening Lily was getting ready for the actual performance of the pantomime. She had fetched a new lollipop from the police station in secret.

'It isn't the same. But I'll get used to it,' Lily sniffed. And I know I did the right thing, she thought.

Bravely, Lily put on her costume. Then she put on extra sparkly earrings. And she dressed up the new lollipop as a wand. Now she was ready. So was everyone else. The headmistress was dressed as an ugly sister. She wished everyone luck. The opening music began. The curtain went up. The show was on.

Cinderella sat sadly in the hearth. Her ugly sisters went off to the ball. And Cinderella was left alone, wishing. Now Lily came on. She took a deep breath. She tried not to think about the old lollipop. She tried not to wonder if it had gone to a good home. She concentrated.

'You shall not stay here in the hearth after all,' she chanted. 'No, instead you shall go to the prince's great ball. Fetch me some mice.'

Cinderella fetched the mice. She put down the cage and Lily waved her lollipop over it.

'To change you to a horse I firmly wish,' she said, 'with a rippling mane and a tail that goes swish.'

The lights went out. Everyone waited. But nothing happened. There was no flash. No horse came on instead. Lily stood very still. She went on waiting.

'Have another go,' whispered Cinderella. 'Try again.'

'To change you to a horse I firmly wish,' said Lily loudly, 'with a rippling mane and a tail that goes swish.'

Still nothing happened. There was a deadly silence. Then, in the wings, Lily thought she heard someone giggling.

Then on to the stage crept Sammy and Susie Squiffins. Lily could just see them. They stood in the gloom. They seemed to be holding something between them.

'Go on. You say it,' whispered Sammy.

'No, you,' said Susie.

'No, you,' said Sammy.

There was more giggling. Then they began to chant something together.

'She's got the wrong wand. Oh, dear, how tragic,' they sang.

What? thought Lily. This isn't in the script. This isn't what we practised.

Then Sammy got hold of Lily's new lollipop. Gently he pulled it out of her hand. Susie slipped something else in its place. And as Lily's hand closed round it they sang, 'That one didn't work, 'cos it's this one that's magic.'

5 **The Magic Lollipop**

Lily stood still as a statue. In her hand was her trusty old lollipop. She knew it straight away, even in the dark. She knew it even though Sammy and Susie had dressed it up as a wand again. She would know that lollipop anywhere. But she didn't know how it had got there. She thought she was dreaming.

'Go on,' said Cinderella. 'Try the words again now.'

Lily pulled herself together. She said the words for the third time. And now there was a flash. Away went the mice and on came the horse. The lights came up and everyone clapped. They clapped and clapped. Some cheered. And still Lily didn't know what to make of it all.

But she concentrated. She turned Lennie's pumpkin into a carriage. She turned Cinderella's rags into the beautiful dress. Cinderella went to the ball. And the curtain came down at the end of the first half.

Lily walked into the wings. Sammy and Susie stood there grinning proudly.

'We bought it back,' announced Sammy.

'With our pocket money,' said Susie.

Lily shook her head. She still thought she was dreaming.

'A rich American man bought it first,' explained Susie. 'He wrote out a cheque for hundreds of pounds. So your lollipop will give hundreds of presents to hundreds of children, Lily.'

Lily nodded. She understood that. That was wonderful news.

'But then we asked the man if we could buy it back for you,' said Sammy. 'We didn't think he'd let us. But we thought it was worth a try. And he looked at us for a long time. Then he said "Yes".'

'He said he was touched,' said Susie. 'He paid a lot of money for your lollipop. But he still had lots left. But if we gave up all our money we wouldn't have any left. That was real giving, he said.'

'So he sold it to us for four pounds twenty-five,' said Sammy. 'He put that in the fund for children in need too. And he said he was really proud to have owned your lollipop even just for half an hour.'

Lily clutched the precious lollipop shakily in one hand. And with the other arm she gave Sammy and Susie a big hug. Large tears of happiness started to smudge her makeup.

'I'm very proud of you,' she croaked. 'And I'm very touched too,' she sniffed.

The second half of the pantomime went beautifully after that. Cinderella ran away from the ball. The prince found her slipper. Then he found Cinderella again too. At the very end Lennie, the retired lollipop man from over the hill, came on dressed as Father Christmas. Lily thrust her lollipop in front of his sleigh.

'Stop! Children,' she cried. Then Lennie climbed out and asked the children what they wanted for Christmas.

'We've always wanted a pet,' said Sammy and Susie. 'But our dad's funny about pets,' they added sadly.

Oh, if only they could have a pet, thought Lily. They deserve one; and she twirled her lollipop without really meaning to.

And at that very moment a tiny kitten frisked on to the stage. It had escaped from the caretaker's house. The caretaker was looking for homes for six kittens.

The kitten ran straight to Sammy and Susie. It curled up between them and purred. Sammy and Susie stroked it longingly.

'But Dad would never let us keep it,' they said sadly.

Lily stared hard at Mr Squiffins. She twirled the lollipop again.

'Wouldn't I?' said Mr Squiffins. He gave Lily a big wink. 'Now what makes you think that?' And he picked up the kitten and placed it in Sammy's arms.

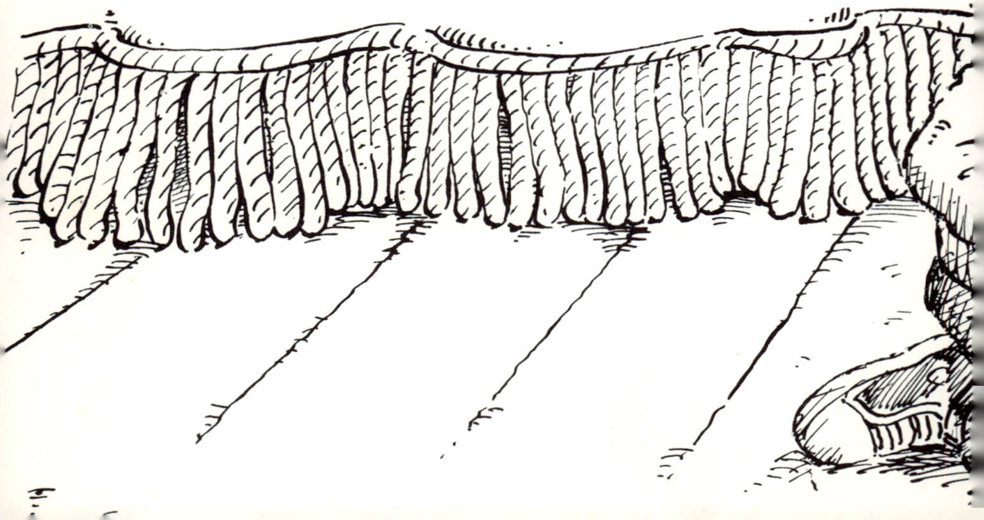

Sammy and Susie were surprised and thrilled. So was Lily. She felt a little weak. She slipped outside for some air.

'Oh, lollipop,' she said. 'You must have even more magic in you than I thought.'

She thought of happy children opening presents on Christmas morning. From in the school she heard squeaks as Sammy and Susie cuddled their new kitten.

Lily squeezed her lollipop tightly. She stared at it in wonder. And the big silver star on top gleamed back in the moonlight.